AF227824

To my family and my little girls for all the memories of playing the Animal Guessing Game.

Animals

Oh!

Hi there! I didn't see
you.
My name is Dot.

What's your name?

Animals

Nice to meet you.
I love to play games.
In fact, I was about to play
a game right now.

Would you like to play with
me?

Animals

Great!!

Then turn the page
and
let's get started!

Animals

Let's play an animal guessing game.
I'll give three clues of an animal that I'm thinking about, and you guess which animal.

Are you ready?
Are you sure? Do you need to have a snack or use the washroom?

Great! Let's get started.

Animals

This animal is really, really, big.

It swims in the ocean
And it sprays water from
the top of it's head.

Do you know
which animal
I'm thinking of?

If you guessed a whale, you're...
CORRECT!!

**The Blue whale is the largest whale and
they, like us, breathe air.
They have a blowhole on top of their
heads and they come up to the
surface of the water and
breath through their blowhole.
Whales can stay underwater
up to 90 mins.
What an amazing animal!!**

Animals

Ok, Next animal...

This animal is also really, big
and walks on land.
It's grey in colour
And has a long trunk that can
spray water.

Which animal am I thinking of?

An Elephant!!

Elephants are the largest land
animal
in the world.
Did you know that elephants
can't jump and they eat about
16 hours a day.
That's a lot of food.
Are you having fun?? I sure am.
Let' guess another animal.

Animals

This animal is a bird and
is often near water.
It can fly and swim
And says,

QUACK! QUACK!

QUACK!
QUACK!

A DUCK!!

Great job! You are such an animal expert.

Did you know that ducks see very well underwater? And they eat seeds, fruit and small insects. It's true!

Animals

Alright, last animal.

This animal is big and scary.
It lives on the flat lands with
their pride,
And they are known as the
King of the jungle.

Any Guesses?!?

A LION!!
You are the best!!!

The lion is part of the cat family.
They are the only cats that live in groups.
Their pride or group can have up to 30 lions and the females are the main hunters.

Animals

That was a great game.

Did you have fun?
Great!
Well, I must go, but keep
an eye out for me and we can
play more games!!
Thank you for playing with me.

See you again!

Animals

Draw your favorite animal and find 3 facts about it.

Now it's your turn!

Gather family and friends and play the Animal Guessing Game!

See how many animals you can guess.

Good Luck!!

Collect, FUN with DOT books
The book series that let's you play along!

Other books by Jessie Bairos-Retsas

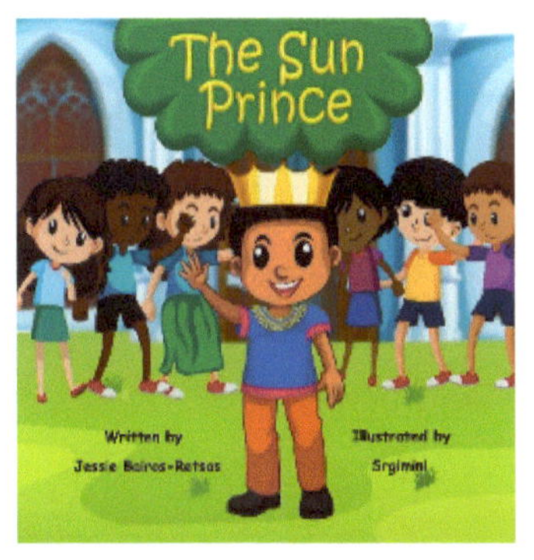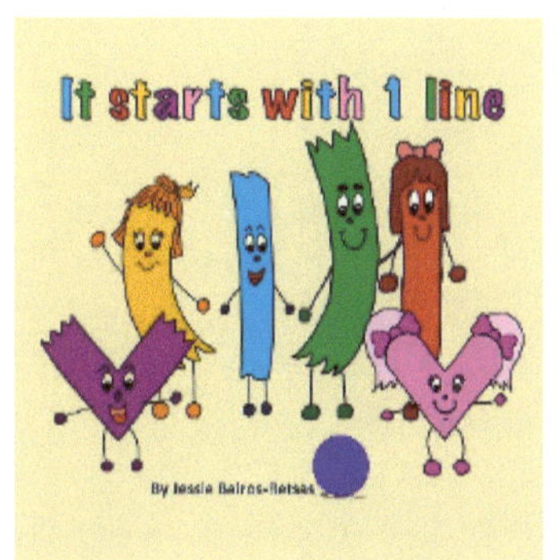

Order your copy on Amazon.
Please leave reviews